A NIHILIST WALKS
INTO A BAR

A NIHILIST WALKS
INTO A BAR

Brianna Ferguson

Mansfield Press

Library and Archives Canada Cataloguing in Publication

Title: A nihilist walks into a bar / Brianna Ferguson.
Names: Ferguson, Brianna, author.
Description: Poems.
Identifiers: Canadiana 20210340428 | ISBN 9781771262750 (softcover)
Classification: LCC PS8611.E7374 N54 2021 | DDC C811/.6—dc23

Editor for the Press: Stuart Ross
Cover Design: Marshall Reeves
Author Photo: Brittany Ferguson
Typesetting: Denis De Klerck

The publication of *A Nihilist Walks Into a Bar* has been generously supported by
the Canada Council for the Arts and the Ontario Arts Council.

Mansfield Press Inc.
25 Mansfield Avenue, Toronto, Ontario, Canada M6J 2A9
Publisher: Denis De Klerck
www.mansfieldpress.net

For Charlie

CONTENTS

JUST WORDS

I want to be the first person to
truly believe that SodaStream
can replace everything.
One could argue the bubbles
are like the crunch of chips,
the bottle makes it like beer,
the zero-cal flavour shots are like
actual flavour, so what the hell
else do you need?
One could argue such things
in this world where the earth
can be argued flat and vaccines
dangerous. With words,
all things can be accomplished.
If enough people
believe something, how
can it not be true?

The Voice of God

Pets are afraid of vacuums, yes,
but every time I haul out Big Red
my dog looks at me like "Brianna Ferguson –"
she always uses my full name
"– Brianna Ferguson, I thought we were done with this"
and I say yes but sometimes life forces you
to do things you'd rather not.
All she hears is "Mmm fmm fmm,"
then the vacuum starts shouting its
universal language of hate and aggression.
Soon she's out the door, trembling
in the backyard with the poop and the snow.
This happens weekly, and
she'll never understand it. Her whole life
she'll try to avoid the inevitable,
cower in fear, pray it doesn't happen,
then lose her mind when it does.
Meanwhile, I'll keep telling her
"It's okay, baby" in a language
she can't understand,
she'll keep thinking me cruel, and
I'll keep thinking her a coward,
and that's the world
we live in.

CHRISTIAN CAMP

The counsellors all had fake names –
to protect them against stalking
after they'd saved everybody's soul.
How do you *not* stalk the hot guy
or girl who saved you from the flames of hell?

Your counsellor was called Nanners –
the most phallic of the fruit nicknames.
A derivative of Anna, she had a strong chin,
hair longer and straighter than yours would ever be,
and a green hoodie with thumb holes punched through
the tips of the sleeves.
Conscious or not,
an adorable attempt
at a fleece stigmata.

You watched her buck teeth beseeching God
to bless your Jell-O as you peeked
at the other heathens who wouldn't
shut their eyes before the lord.
You spent all day on the archery range
and in the lake, thinking of things to confess
around the campfire – anything
to keep her all to yourself
a little longer.

She gave you Matthew 7:7
– knock, and it shall be opened unto you –
and you wondered if she wanted you
to knock on her cabin door
after hours.

One day, she disappeared
with your best friend
for an hour-long walk, and
for the first time you knew
what it was to hate someone.

When your friend got back, you cornered her,
asked what they had talked about
– knowing, somehow, they'd spent the afternoon
kissing in a sunlit grotto.

Your friend shrugged,
        said, "Boys,"
and you tried to let it go.

On the last day, Nanners hugged everyone goodbye.
For you –
        it wasn't your imagination –
she lingered the longest.
                        "Don't stop
seeking Him," she said, holding your hands
in her own.

As you pulled away, you saw her
out the back of the bus. She was kissing Brad
        (or Bingo)
by the mess hall,
                        his hands knocking hard
on the door
        of her godly ass.

In the Garden

The old lady of Monday afternoon
            keeps watch
                        in the park
with her military-grade binoculars.

The birds of the swamp
            are active today –
heads dripping gutter water
            as spring cracks its
                        leather whip
at their downy backs.

From five hundred metres
            she can hardly see their colours.
            Just black-and-white forms,
            male and female,
            tagging each other like
                        wedding gifts in a registry.

There is so much sex,
            so many flapping bits,
it stands to reason that boy birds,
            cousins, brothers, mothers, and sons
            are sometimes tripped
            by the wires of incestual sins.
Older birds take younger birds
            without their consent,
            choking them in the beaver fever water
as they seek survival
            through their progeny.

But all this woman sees
            from this distance is
God's creatures
            in the Garden.

The Wanting

You tell me I'm still young, but
a young body doesn't pop
or snap this much just
sitting on the couch,
reaching for the phone.

You tell me
there's still shit to look forward to
but you can't name a single movie
where the real story starts
once the main character's
already married with a career
and a hobby and all the stamps
they ever wanted to have
in their passport.

Yes, I'm complaining
I have everything I wanted.
I just never realized
all I really wanted
was to keep on wanting.

QUITZILLA

I like the Quitzilla app
because you're always winning.
Whenever you started stopping
whatever wonderful thing
was ruining your life
it counts that as like 90% of the journey
toward some random goal.
Did you stop drinking five minutes ago?
Jesus, you're already
97% of the way to the six-minute mark!
Three whole days under your belt?
Holy fuck, that's almost four!
The little meter refreshes
every few seconds with
another percentage point, and
it's like, okay I can definitely do this.
Like the first single-cell whatsit
swimming in its own primordial filth,
you can become a person
again. Yes, it's tedious, but
how many millions of years did it take
to get from single cells to us?
And look how fucked-up
we still are.

THE DANGEROUS

My dog looks cutest
when she's curled into a perfect circle,
her nose tucked into her asshole.
The number of people who will lick
a sidewalk condom is zero, but
the number of people
who will let my dog lick them in the mouth
after she's licked a sidewalk condom is
definitely not zero. There's no way
I could even touch the flusher
on a floor-model toilet
without washing my hands.
One time, my uncle licked
the elevator buttons in the hospital
to show me I shouldn't fear germs.
He didn't die, but
a part of me did.
So many dangers are all in your head.
That doesn't mean they can't kill you.

STORIED

I always feel like a champion
of women's rights
when I don't wear makeup
while alone and unseen in my trailer.
As I shovel the driveway, naked
of face, I'm certain the paparazzi
are in Rick and Marilyn's bushes,
or hiding behind the backhoe Matt uses
to plow the trailer park. And I'm like
here I am, fellas. Take a good look
at a real woman.
I won't usually receive any calls or commendations,
but I know somewhere out there,
a starry-eyed little fourteen-year-old girl
is choosing a book
instead of mascara
or some shit and
it's all because of my plainness.
Butterfly effect and all that.
I'm not saying appearance is nothing.
Just that I'm less interested in the tattoo
than the story behind why you got it.

LACUNA

Last night (Christmas) we fought
about my drinking and
went to bed in that way where
you try not to touch each other, but
you're in the same bed, so
how the hell is that supposed to work?
You said it's insane I wanted a Christmas beer
when six days ago I was like
please help me stop drinking forever.
Forever isn't Friday. Forever might not even
be real. Certainly not real
for humans. You said
no one has any memory
once they're feeling good,
and all I thought was
you're right,
everything I can remember is
sad. Wouldn't it be nice
not to remember anything? When you're a kid,
Christmas can't come fast enough.
Do you remember being a child? Apparently,
I can't even remember Sunday.

FUTURE PARENTS

This is the last decade
I'll be young.
In seven years, I'll be forty
and nothing I do will be remarkable
for my age.

Today we went for a walk
and talked about adoption.
Then we watched *Godzilla 2000*
and you asked if I liked it.
I said I was glad
you shared it with me
and you were like
don't talk to me like
I'm a child.

I tried to google
Star Trek: The Next Generation porn
in an incognito window after
I had a sex dream about Levar Burton, and
I had to go through a CAPTCHA
proving I was human.
I guess humans don't google
that sort of thing much anymore.

Anyway, you think we could be parents,
but we don't even have groceries or
an answer to why we're alive.

CONTRARIAN

The heaviest I ever got
was on my wedding day.
This was after I spent $40
to join a weight-loss pool and
ended up gaining six pounds.
I'm not a contrarian –
I'd follow almost any rule
on a sign or spoken
by a face with a title, but
expectations are different.
The whole world knows brides
want to be skinny on their wedding day.
That's a thing we know, the way
we all used to know
there was a god and
a book that could tell you
how to live.
I used to know that, and then
one day I knew the opposite, and
I'd be lying if I said
it wasn't a relief.

The Greatest Thing

It had been dark for days
       when I found myself
annoyed
       the sun was in my eyes, and
I couldn't see YouTube.

The sky was on its knees,
       apologizing, and
I just wanted to watch
       a girl with short bangs
              cover "Creep."

By the time I remembered to open the blinds,
it was dark again.

The Bible says
       I'm the greatest thing
              the universe has got
                     to offer.
The movies say
       I'm barely a human woman if
              I don't bleach
                     my asshole.

Definitely
it's somewhere
between the two, but
who's to say where?

Oops

I went for two walks today
and saw
no one under the age of eighty.

I tried not to buy
a small bag of chips,
then bought
a large bag of chips
and ate most of it.

I'm wondering how many calories
I'm burning by typing this.

Q-TIPS

The whole world is just
people making Q-tips
and saying,
now don't put those
in your ears.

*

One time I climbed the Eiffel Tower
and all I could think about was
how badly I had to pee and
how I'd forgotten my lip balm
on a bed
in Belgium.

*

Twelve roads feed the roundabout
at the Arc de Triomphe, and
the only way it works is
if anything bad happens,
everyone's at fault.

WILD

In quarantine, I walk from
window to window, like
there's something to see
just past the edges of
what's in front of me.
My grandma used to cry
with joy when I'd call her.
Back then, I thought a call
from me wasn't much, so
I didn't do it often. But
that was before I, too, was
95 and sitting all day
in my house, wondering why
I didn't go wild
when I had the chance.

LUXURY

It's such a luxury
to shout
fuck it
I could die
tomorrow.

Some people actually
will die
tomorrow, and
I doubt
it's any easier
for them to
ask out their crushes.

Pass the Time

Because I'm me
I spend my days discussing
whether a line in a poem
wouldn't be better in all caps,
or if perhaps
lowercase would communicate
a more profound truth.
Everyone does something and
this is what I do.
I also drink too much
and go through more crackers
than an elementary school.

You can run a country or
debate font sizes, and
one day the sun will explode
and not even the debris
will remember that time
after you'd just become a teacher,
when you told a whole class
honour roll was spelled
honour role, and then cried
in the copy room.

THE REBEL ATTENDS A WRITERS' RETREAT

You sit at the old table made of reclaimed pew wood, etched in
the coffee rings of so many mugs that came before yours. There's
a hushed, churchy feel as you type poems that have nothing to
do with the woods. The cottage is in the woods, and the thoughts
in your head are meant to be woodsy, but retreats have always
turned you on, made your mind fidget like you did in the itchy
leotards and lace dresses your mom crammed you into for
church. Squirming, your mind on anything but god, you always
looked for money beside the hymnals. But all you found was
Werther's wrappers. Writing about fucking, about beer, about the
insatiable roar of an intersection in downtown Vancouver, you
think only of the time a man walked down a crowded sidewalk
with a contraption made of several bent coat hangers twisted
together. He gouged your ankles and the ankles of everyone
around you for no reason you could think of – nothing beyond
doing with hangers what you're not supposed to do.

The Sitters

They sit us down in the crib
and tell us everything out there
will kill you
if you let it.
So don't let it.

They sit us down on the potty
and say if you don't go here
no one will want
to be your friend.

They sit us down on the plastic chairs,
say stay here and don't speak
without raising your hand.

They sit us down on the bus,
tell us don't switch seats,
don't move when the bus is moving,
don't talk too loud and you'll get home safe.

They sit us down in classrooms,
say this is your future, and
if you don't want to sit here
for the next thirteen years
you'll never amount to anything.

They sit us down in offices
and say if you don't stay here
you won't be able to pay rent
or hydro, or the car dealership,
or the gas, or monthly parking, and
you'll live carless and hungry in the dark.

They sit us down in the rooms where people listen
and we share how unfulfilled we are, how confused,
and they hand over bottles with sleepy-time pills
so we can sit up in bed,
not quite awake,
not quite asleep.

They stand us up,
guts bulging, heartbeats dim,
say all that sitting will kill you,
you're wasting your life.

      And then,
not much later
they come, heads bowed,
charts in hands,
say you might want to sit down
for this.

ERIN BROCKOVICH

Sixteen and still prepubescent
I am watching *Erin Brockovich*.
A woman is crying in her bed
asking Erin if she's still a woman without
a uterus or breasts.

I stretch my legs out to ease
the tension in my groin, where
the testes we have yet to find
settle down like shaken goose eggs
in their round and terrible reality.

With no prying high school eyes in sight,
I let the blanket slide down my flat chest.
Mom's double Ds pinch under her arms
as she reaches for the M&Ms.
The lips that said, "We'll ask again in a year
if nothing happens," are sticky and blue.
Nothing being my period.
Nothing being my tits and
all the usual armour of a teenage girl.
Nothing has happened. Nothing hangs
off me like an unbloodied sheet.

"Can you imagine?" Mom mutters
as the pretty woman smiles.

Erin's kids are home with the guy next door.
Bored, she pinches the bridge of her nose
with a finger twice the size of my cunt.

TONGUES

The church is in a half-circle building that looks like an old airplane hangar. "That's how I knew it was real," says the friend who brought me here. "Phony churches are all about the presentation, but this place – you can tell it's about God, not the fancy sound system." A bald, red-faced man stands at the podium, shouting that God will give you what you want, if only you believe hard enough. Unless He doesn't, in which case it's because what you wanted didn't fit with His plan. But be sure to pray anyway. The sermon is shapeless and boring as if the guy had an idea but didn't write anything down. I start planning my escape, and suddenly the preacher's saying words that aren't words, and the people around me are raising their hands, saying non-words of their own. "What is this?" I ask the friend. "Tongues," she says. "It happens when you're too full of the Holy Spirit." "You mean, when you can't understand him?" "Yeah." When the tongues are finished, and the prayer leaders descend among us, I ask a woman with phony red hair and smoker's teeth whether I could pray hard enough that God would give me the reproductive organs he left out while he was making me in the womb. The woman looks taken aback, blinks, unsure perhaps, until she nods hard and says, "Well, yes! Of course! If you pray hard enough!" I must seem unconvinced, because next she asks if I've ever spoken in tongues, if I'd like to give it a try. "Well sure!" I say. "Who wouldn't want to be so full of god, he's literally exploding out of their mouth?" She presses a hand on my belly, looks me in the eyes. "It'll come from your stomach," she says. "You'll feel it churning there first, then you just open your mouth." I close my eyes and listen as she prays with more non-words. Nothing happens, but I hear people going quiet beside me, which means they're watching me. So, always one to please, I start speaking gibberish, which is surprisingly easy. She presses harder, as if looking for a fetal heartbeat. "That's it," she says. "Let Him fill you up." I don't know if my gibberish wasn't convincing enough, but I never did get those Fallopian tubes, or that uterus or ovaries. Maybe they were just against God's plan.

Sober Truth

Last night we made beeswax candles
with wax from our own hive.
       I don't know what else people do
       at night when they're not drinking.
We spent hours refining and melting and
pouring the wax, and when we went to light one,
the whole thing burned up in two seconds.
Like the organic deodorant
I used when I was eighteen and terrified
of breast cancer. The deo didn't
do anything and neither did the candle
and I guess that's why we developed
all those chemicals that are killing the earth.
Fresh armpits and scented candles
might seem small
against the whole world, but
have you ever sat in a smelly room
or gone to school with BO?

STARDUST MEANS SPACE GARBAGE

What will we remember of our time here
asks the poem on the bus banner.
My eyes flit to the ad for abortion clinics
before drifting back to the question.

Yvonne is the poet's name.
She tells me we're made of stardust and soil,
that the shadows may be dark at times,
but you can always shine your way out!

A woman plops down beside me.
She smells like a sidewalk piss and
looks like a Florida tent city.

I straighten up and my backpack digs
a finger into my windpipe.
I push it to the floor and try to ignore
the sound of my mason jar water bottle
blowing its load over my laptop.

At the next stop, thirty-five
private-school kids get on,
laughing that one among them
doesn't know where McGill is.
They say he'll end up in Sprott-Shaw –
my first alma mater.

My car is rusting in a field in my hometown.
I owe fifty thousand dollars to faceless people
who don't care if I figure out how to be a teacher
so long as I figure out how to pay them back.

The bus comes to a stop and
it's finally raining hard enough for an umbrella.
I unzip my bag, pull out the soggy apparatus,
which flops limp at my touch.
It's a ten-minute walk to class,
but it might as well be an hour.

THE DROWNING

The crying girl who knew him
won't say anything beyond
"I thought he was joking around."

The lake glints in the evening sun
like a thousand butts in a crystal ashtray
refusing to go out. Search-and-rescue boats
are slumped in the harbour,
blue lights blinking their mantra.

In the parking lot sits his Jeep
still warm from the mid-July sun.
A drink sits in the cup holder,
his fingerprints like sandy
footprints on the aluminum.
The phone with the text saying
he's headed to the beach
lies tossed in the back with the runners.

A hundred metres down the beach,
radios shriek, children splash.
Snacks are sold, beers are popped.
The untouched majority hold on to
their towels, their inflatable swans,
as the rescue helicopter rises,
empty.

IMPOSSIBLE TO WASTE

I sat on the couch today
from when I woke up till
now, when
I'm about to make supper.
      I got up a few times for coffee,
but it's been raining all day, and
there's been nothing to
hold my attention beyond
the confines of my blanket and
the dog asleep in the crook of my leg.
      I gave a couple hours to Duolingo,
learning French I may never use,
but that was it.

Once, years ago,
      I lost a whole day
learning the Cyrillic alphabet.
I'd seen Angelina Jolie in *Salt*
and thought Russian was the sexiest language.
I learned every letter and
a few basic expressions.
      We lived in Vancouver then,
and it had been raining for days
as it's been raining here.
I never used the Russian, though,
and a week or two later
it was gone.

If I'm honest, though,
      I don't remember how I've spent
      most of my days,
      regardless of what I did.

My husband once said to me
after a bland and meaningless day at work,
    if nothing means anything
    in any cosmic sense,
    then nothing matters any less
    or any more than anything else.

Which, if you can
stomach it, really takes
the pressure off.

YOUTH GROUP WEEKEND RETREAT

They took us to a cabin on top of a mountain –
like Jesus when he went
to the woods to be tempted.

There was a woman there I'd never seen before.
Her bible was in a leather case
       with a zipper
and she had special highlighters
you could use on the onion-skin paper
       without bleeding through.
She told me where to get the highlighters
and I went the first chance I got.

I found my own zipper case, and a TNIV bible
that was supposed to be better
than the version I had.
I searched through the CDs and hoodies,
the stuffed animals and the books
explaining the bible, but
I couldn't find the highlighters.

In the end,
I got a generic one at the dollar store.
I highlighted "in the beginning,
god created the heavens and the earth"
just to try it out, and sure as hell,
it bled through to "god looked on all
he had made, and was disgusted, for
       the hearts of man were wicked"
on the very next page.

A few years later, when I moved
to my first apartment,
I gave the bible to the Salvation Army,
along with the pants and shirts I'd gotten
too big to wear.

FUTILITY

I am sober and trying
to mark English papers while
sanding my heels with
80 grit sandpaper.
On the cushion beside me,
my dog is licking her asshole.
Really getting in there, like
one day
it might finally be clean.

TREK

We were watching our third
Star Trek episode of the day
when you asked if
I'm a lesbian.
All I'd said was
Kristen Stewart called herself gay
in an interview, and
wasn't that cool?
And suddenly
there it was,
like a fart
in the middle of the night.
Obviously not, I said,
But we could both smell
something
on me, and
how do you lie
to a nose?

WHOPPER

Whatever the recommended intake of
medium regular coffees is, I am over
by at least eight different people's
heart attacks.
The McDonald's drive-thru ladies
have known me by name in
every neighbourhood I've lived in.
I wish I could say I go to more drive-thrus
now that they're the only place
we're allowed to be, but
that would be a whopper.
When's the last time someone said
whopper outside of a drive-thru?
When's the last time someone said anything
without using their thumbs?
My favourite weight-loss move is eating
no meals before noon, then
five meals before midnight while
wearing a Fitbit.

GAS LEAK

I know I said I'd help you
write your resumé, but
the truth is I had to sexy dance
to the new T Swift in my window
with peanut butter in the corners
of my mouth. One time I mixed
5% beer with 8% beer and chips
and a whole tub of candy worms, and
my farts were so bad, you thought
there was a gas leak. We were already
married, but I still pretended to
help you look for the leak
rather than tell you the truth.
You might think time makes adults of us all,
    but I don't know
where you got that idea.

CRACK

My neighbour just told me
at 2 p.m.
to have a good night,
which makes sense, because
the sun's going down.

I was out for my morning walk,
trying not to drink
before supper.
I don't know
how many white hairs I have
by now, but probably like forty.

I'm a year older
than Taylor Swift and I have nine
fewer hit albums.
On the cover of her latest,
her blond hair is perfectly
braided and definitely not
turning white. I don't know how
it always feels like a whole workday
has gone by no matter the hour
you crack that first beer,
but somehow it always does.

NARCISSUS

I was at the gym, and a woman
in the change room had her boobs out
as I walked in. I smiled hello, but
with my mask on, she couldn't tell.
I squinted my eyes to let her know
I was smiling, but I'm sure it just looked like
I was trying *really* hard
to see her boobs from far away.

They say the brain is the universe's way
of knowing itself, but
could the universe really just want
to stare at its own boobs?

There's a book about this
somewhere, I'm sure, but
I'll never read it.

The Fearful

I don't understand people
      who listen to their own TVs at
      record low volume, as if
      they can't enjoy something
      without challenging themselves.
Some people can't let their guards down
      at any time of day.
Some people sleep with baseball bats and
      loaded guns within reach.
If someone came into my house to kill me
      I would definitely die.

One time an American who used to be my uncle
      handed me a loaded Glock
      and didn't tell me it was loaded. I guess
      just to see what would happen?
He told me the Mexicans are coming for
      what we have, and we need
      to be ready.
He used to drive for days to attend festivals
      just for people who like motorcycles.

The other day, I read hundreds of people got Covid
      at a biker festival in the States.

I wonder how many leather vests hid Glocks
      as everyone shook hands and chatted about the
      pansy-ass libs letting their lives
      be controlled by fear.

TEACHERS' RETREAT

Hanging on the doors in the bathroom stalls,
posters advertise a wellness retreat for
teachers who've lost their way.
A man stands at the sea, arms spread.
Smiling women hold children, which is odd because
we're not allowed to touch the students.
The colours are all yellows and blues,
soft like bathrobes, like May sunshine, like
a relaxing piss in a private stall.
The phone number on the posters is
not called Helpline, but
If You'd Like To Book A Consultation,
as if they're advertising weight loss
or hair treatment, not
the slow death of a career.

In the stall downstairs, someone has ripped
one of the numbers off. I try to find this person
in the halls. I look for a drooping face, pallid skin,
perhaps a deadening in the eyes that says
help me, please, I have lost my way.
But all the eyes I see look the same,
and soon I give up the search.

Parts Girl

The first job was delivering car parts
to shady garages in my hometown.
The cars were stock – no air conditioning –
with engines that rattled and screamed
from years of neglect.
The warehouse was rank with clogged,
uncleanable oil, steel-toed shoes, dusty, collapsing
boxes of old parts, and the smoky, stooped figures
of the recent grads, the recovering addicts, and
the other Lost who worked there.

The walls of the garages were draped in calendars
of scantily clad women. Men stood
and watched from fart-filled coveralls
as we pulled up to drop off their rotors
and brake pads. Our eighteen- and nineteen-
year-old bodies were draped
in oversize tees that swung just enough
with the effort of picking up parts to hint
at what lay inside.

Sometimes, they'd request specific drivers
to drop off their parts. They picked the parts they liked
as if selecting us from a catalogue.
I was the leggy one. Then there was
the girl with big boobs, the redhead,
the short girl who wasn't much stronger than she looked.
We came to them downtown, uptown, across town, way up
in the mountains, at the ends of dirt roads.
We appeared in our little white cars,
ready to serve. They offered us beer,
as if we hadn't just driven there,
safe in the knowledge
we had to say no.

And between garages, we rolled down our windows,
blasted music, thought about driving
past the outskirts of town, all the while
heading back to the warehouse,
our minimum wages, our
numbered spaces, as loyally as tools
and oils and filters to their boxes.

Teachers in Summer

We are the teachers with our white calves and
pastel summer clothes. We stand in lines
at the bank and chit-chat with the widows
out to kill an afternoon.
We pay for parking downtown where we scoff
at the lazy, reckless youth wandering around
as we lick plain vanilla cones.
Too poor to dine out,
to travel beyond the next town,
we sleep late and sip coffee from favourite mugs.
Our dreamt-of summer projects lie unfinished,
unpurchased, unlearned on concrete floors
in half-finished garages. We bump
into students at the supermarket and
talk too long, oscillating between casual conversation
and a last stab at imparting wisdom.
We fall asleep early on porches
beside glasses of wine gone warm.
The mosquitoes peck at our aging bodies
take lazy sips and fly off buzzed.
Everyone says *my god you're so lucky,*
I wish I got summers off.

Then they pause:
but don't you get bored?

E.I.

The Employment Insurance pays
two thousand a month.
The mortgage is seven hundred and ten dollars.
The car, two hundred and sixty.
Insurance is one hundred and seventy-seven dollars.
The utilities, three hundred and something.
The phone is sixty-seven. Gas food beer
and new underwear take up the rest.
There's no room to move in this
government-issued waiting room of an income,
so I sit here not drinking, going for walks and
waiting for brilliance to fill my mind –
the only place that costs nothing.
There are just two options for work
if I wanted to work. I could be a teacher like I trained for,
teaching subjects I did not train for, and in which
I have no interest. Or I could work in a dollar store or
gas station making less than the government pays me
to do nothing at all. Every two weeks
when I fill out the reports that
give me more money,
I have to answer a series of questions.
Have you attended school?
Have you left the country?
Have you made any money at all?
They show me my answers before I hit Submit.
All the No's cascade down the monitor
in a neat little row.
Two more weeks gone by with only No's
to mark the many things that
might have happened to me.
The money is mostly spent
by the end of the first day,

then I have to sit tight until
thirteen more days have passed.
It's a boring business being nothing at all,
but it's better, I guess,
than being something awful.

THE MAID

I once worked four days as a housekeeper
at a prominent hotel
in my hometown.
Let me start by saying
if you have never chiselled a stranger's
dehydrated piss and travellers' diarrhea
from a toilet bowl in forty-degree weather
with your hair in your eyes,
you might not know misery.

There was a woman there
who told me, pressing her hand
to her chest as if in oath, that
cleaning was her passion.
"I just want a cleaner world," she said,
her voice grown rough from
the half pack of cigarettes she smoked every shift.
The sadness in her faded brown eyes
as she fought to convince the both of us
was enough to put me in my car
and on the road to the university.

Five years later, though, there I was
again, bent double, chiselling
ignorance from the minds of
high school students, scrubbing
phones from fingers and
laziness from growing bodies.
Only now, the rooms were freezing,
the hair in my eyes
half grey.

THE GATEHOUSE

My collar is grey polyester and broken cardboard
melted through by last season's sweaty necks.
My shoes are clown red and dust – ten dollars
at the place downtown that was forced to close
after the Mexican labour issue.
The ceiling above my head is dotted with
dusty cobwebs that remind me
of nebulae before infrared filters.
There's a mosquito in my ear but I
can't reach it no matter how many times
I hit myself in the head.

People rumble to my window in vehicles
that cost more than my house. They say
they'd like to camp and ask
if I can do something about the bugs.

You must love camping, they say.
I pop a Mentos and hope
they can't smell the Pilsner.

TRAPS

Once a month at the window company
a guy came in to kill the mice
that had wandered into the office
from the warehouse.
He was middle-aged, overweight, soft-spoken.
He used to tell me how he was going
to open a fine menswear place downtown.
You could get two good Italian suits
for the price of one. The men would be served whisky
and the women served wine. He had the building
picked out, the down payment saved up
        from a lifetime killing tiny creatures.

I wished him well, tried not to listen
whenever the traps sprang shut over fragile,
furry necks.

        Or when the local news said only a few months later
that his shop was already going under.

He came back not long after that to resume killing.
He didn't stop to talk anymore. Death hung off him
like his now-baggy uniform. Mice came,
their necks broke, and they went out
to the dumpster in his tired hands.

BURIED WIRES

Then there was the office job for the couple
about to divorce. Their garage was the office, and
the only bathroom was in their house.
I'd walk through the kitchen, and
on the table I'd see a bottle of Bacardi
and a note saying something like
here you go, asshole,
I hope the two of you are
very happy together.

It was his house and his company,
and his parents lived in the carriage house.
Sometimes his mother would sit on a stool behind me
and complain about his wife. Why was Stacy so mean,
when all they'd ever given her was love?

Sometimes I'd have to wait to leave,
because Stacy was blocking me in
as she cried in her car. Other times,
I'd stay late to meet with one of their lawyers
and witness something official and damning.

I only lasted two months, and
I hardly remember what the job was.

Something in construction, I think.
Something about locating all the buried wires
and gas lines in the ground
so you don't blow yourself up
when you go to dig a hole.

Follow Your Passion

I love animals and
I need a job, you say.
      So work at a vet's office, they reply.
      Follow your passion and
      you'll never work a day in your life.
And you do.
You go to school,
spend money you don't have and
too many of the few years you do
and then when you finally make it
you discover you're the one
who has to put the animals down.

You go to work and kill animals
from Monday to Friday.
Most people who think only a bit
about animals
kill zero animals.
While you who love them
kill thousands.

People ask what you do.
You say *vet*.
They say *wow*
you must really love animals.

Then they get a look in their eye –
a helping look. They say something like
my niece loves animals and wants
to be a vet one day.
Do you have any advice for her?
      But, of course, they're not really asking.
They already know
what you're going to say.

TRIVIAL

I sit at home
thinking
horrible things all day,
like how
Alex Trebek just died
and now
all that trivia
folded up like love notes in his brain
is starting to rot.
What good is a life
spent
gathering facts
if cancer can just
come along and
wipe the board clean
whenever it wants?
You can argue
the point is to share things learned
with others,
but
what happens
when the last trivial wrinkle is ironed flat,
and there's no one left
to ask any questions?

Having Lived

And no,
since you ask,
they never did
run away
to the woods.

They stayed
and they made it
and then
their lives
were over.

GENIUS

I am reading
Bob Dylan's *Chronicles Volume One* and wondering
if thirty-two and married
is too late
to be a folksinger living in the back of a club,
eating off customers' plates.
I could be radical, I think,
as I scrub the bathroom I own and
play with the dog I own on the floor I own.
I could trade a locked door and
car payments for genius.

I think this,
and then my husband
cleans all his hobby shit
off the counter where it's been for a month
and I'm like, okay no
this is as good as it gets.

STARLET

The YouTube ladies come with their
vintage hairstyles, red lipstick and
dresses, to sing sweet songs in
sweet voices. Their bright rooms
are filled with more light than
my whole house when all the windows
are open. Their uncalloused fingers
press guitar strings soft as May
grasses. If these girls are poems,
then I'm a brochure for a logging college
or plumbing college or something else
unnecessary, not musical, and
best kept off-camera. I sing along
in a rusty tenor, hair bunned, jeans
faded, plucking my uke with blistered
fingers, wondering what my shtick
will be when I launch my channel and
how I'll handle all the press.

The Shut-Ins

I was visiting my parents, which means
sitting on the couch and shouting
over a murder mystery at max volume.
"Why don't you get out and do something,"
I, a thirty-year-old woman with no Saturday plans,
said around a mouthful of Cheezies
into the face of my sixty-year-old mother
in her hand-knitted slippers.

"Don't you owe it to all these murdered women
to get out and live before Dad pushes you
down a manhole and claims you were
out weeding the garden after
chasing your Cheezies with some vodka?"

"And do what?" she asked without turning to look at me.
"Eat dinner? Watch a show?
I'm already doing that."

"I don't know. Get out and meet new people," I said.
"Find something new and beautiful to look at."

"How is that better than this?" she asked.
"The best I could hope for is more of this.
But I'd have to get dressed and buy gas."

The husband was unmasked as the murderer
before I said anything else.
"Is this just all there is, then?" I said.

Mom shrugged, cleaving the bulbous head
from a twisted Cheezie.
"I guess there's always death."

On the TV, the husband was being led away,
his shaved head bowed, toes dragging.

"I'll tell you this," Mom said, "I'd hate to be him.
You think it's boring out here,
imagine being in prison."

BOWLING ALLEYS

You walk into a den of low popcorn ceilings with cobwebbed watermarks. There stand the slouched, nearly extinguished employees, the shabby shoes, the peeling, cracked seats, the bulging waists and unwashed ponytails, linoleum countertops, all of it blinking into existence as your eyes adjust to the dim lights. The bowling alley hiding in the squat building you never notice, with the cracked parking lot, and the claw machine in the foyer with the plastic-eyed carnival cast-off stuffies. Here you find the crooked little people, and no, I don't mean corrupt. The squinting eyes that sell you the lane, the shoes that never go outside, all of it in a tin-can, bell-jar, neither-past-nor-present swirl of neon lights. Like a future imagined by old minds and never realized by the rest of the world. It sits, blinking, as if to say *I didn't actually want any of this. I panicked and went with what I knew I could be. And now more than anything all I want is out.* The developers have their eyes on the land, already looking past the slouched southern wall and garbage in the ditch. But where would the bored people go to fill their Saturday afternoons if it all went away? This white-noise, Muzak place gives so little, but asks so little, and on these weekend days in the hours between drinking, what more could one reasonably want?

Small-Town Saunas

In every small town
          is a public pool.
Attached to this pool
          is a sauna.
Within these saunas
          you will find old white
men. Their chests will be
          hairy, but not like
strongmen in
          black and white,
more like cotton
          fallen from trucks and
lodged in barbed wire.
          Their legs will be slender and
widespread,
          their trunks black,
clamped under bulging bellies.
          They will be talking
about the failures of this
          New World.
The laziness
          of the new generation.
They will express a smouldering
          mistrust of immigrants,
voiced as if
          testing the waters, and
dropped soon after, like a dry pen.

In another time,
          these men, tired, bodies aching from
so many years at the plow,
          would be quiet on the porch, listening
to the breeze. The air would buzz
          with mosquitoes, and the things

that ate them. But here, the air is full
        of the things they say to one another
over the other men with closed eyes,
        and the women who know
how to stay out of it.

The sauna, with its low roof,
        is like the coffin waiting, open-jawed,
        at the end of all of this.
Like the orators of ancient places
        who built nations on words,
these men in the small-town saunas
        have it all figured out.
These men who will shed their trunks
        as soon as they cross the threshold
of the men's change room.
        These men whose balls
will hit the cold water of the toilet and
        make them yelp like kicked dogs.
These men, shivering,
        feeling the cold ground waiting
with dampened coals,
        spread their legs
till their knees almost touch
        one another's.

The coals in the sauna would flare nicely
        if someone dumped water on them,
but a sign on the wall
        asks people not to do this.
And these men did not get where they are
        by disregarding signs.

CLEAN AND WILD

You'd been on this kick for a while where
every part of the yard had a potted plant,
and I just wanted
something of my own.
Something pure and simple, like a
bodhi tree I could lie next to
to write enlightened poems
and flash my bikini bod
to the neighbours.

You had ideas for a ring around the base
to allow for better drainage –
said you could plant a bunch of little flowers,
make it the centrepiece of our yard.

I wanted a dirt mound and a single plant.
I can only love one thing, I said.
I want it clean and wild.

You showed me with firewood
how you'd make a frame,
but even as you laid out the border,
we both knew I'd say no.

I found a cheap lilac
with a bent stem
at the place down the street,
dug a hole and threw it in.
Once it was watered,
I took the dog for a walk
in the swamp downtown.

The grebes were screaming and fucking
in the lake's swelled edges.

I stopped to listen, and
a filthy, mush-mouthed man drinking a Caribou
dragged his bike out of a lilac grove and
started telling me about another time
he saw grebes.
       The whole story was
        I saw grebes another time –
No twist, no moral.

As I scrambled for a phony reason to leave,
I wondered why
I couldn't just say
I came to be alone.

If I can't listen to my own thoughts
in a goddamn swamp
without a man laying his coat
over the natural world
just to hand it back
smelling of him, then
where the hell can I?

LUMPS

I'm always feeling myself up
for lumps and
finding lumps and
calling someone about my lumps.
      The word LUMP is so
      onomatopoeic
of the moment a new one sticks its
fabulous face into the room.
In the comics they write THWACK
when someone's given a what-for, but
the real thing is meatier.

I start googling *what do u do if u find...*
and the search autocompletes with

          A LUMP

robbing me of even that tiny bit of control.

      How can you tell if it's cancerous?
some scared (probably dead now)
fool has typed before me. As if one could gauge
the extent of the destruction bearing down on them
from something as pedestrian
as a little feeling up.

Lumps need special care –
space-age scans, delicate tools and
indifferent interns leaning over microscopes.
They are outside the Band-Aids and Advil
of simple home repair.

It's funny to think something
as beautiful and luscious as

boobs could be so
landminey.
Like Vietnam.

HILARIOUS.

But here we are. Nothing's really free.
Even Diet Coke is worse
than a little tightening of the jeans.

Other gals my age look forward to ultrasounds
for the telltale bump or gash. But
I go to them like a yokel with a LottoMax,
          except
instead of kids or money,
I only want more days.

DOWNTOWN

My buzz wears off as I get off
the train downtown.
I choke on the faces who fill my air
with shapes I don't understand.
Someone's hair is in my mouth.
I'm standing on someone's toes.
A thousand doorknobs present themselves for turning,
dripping in piss and cum and the cracked coughs
of those too stupid or poor to fix them.

Who were these people before this evening?
How did they go from sunrise babies to
smoke in the air,
like '80s photographs of L.A.
before emissions standards?

I turn onto a less-crowded street.
Behind me stands the train station and my
sweltering, empty apartment.
In front of me, the sea
and a sign saying *Do Not Swim.*

On the horizon, ship after ship of plastic things
arrives from countries
a thousand times more crowded than this one.
I could drive to the distant mountains,
but even those are nothing but trails
with colourful signboards
and garbage cans every fifty feet.

THE MUG STORE

I was standing in Chapters and
a man shattered a mug
as I inquired about Louise Glück.

"Umm, could you spell the name,"
the girl asked, glancing worried
at the shattered porcelain.
"G-l-u-c-k," I said, adding
she had just won the Nobel Prize.
"Or maybe it was the Pulitzer –"

"Oh! Well then we *should* have her," she said,
her stubby fingers flying.
The screen flashed several titles,
all of them red.

"Hmm, doesn't look like it,"
her voice at once apologetic and
suspicious of The System.
"Anything else I can help you find?"

She was looking at the man, now bent over,
collecting the shards of the mug.

"Is she any good?" the woman asked,
hurrying away.

"I wouldn't know,"
I called after her.

DINOSAUR PISS

In third grade, we learned that
all the water we have on Earth
is the same water we had
in the time of the dinosaurs.

Realizing what that must mean,
we hit the playground and informed
the first kid with a water bottle
he was drinking dinosaur piss.

The kid took a sip,
shook his head, and said,
"It's not dinosaur piss,
it's human piss." His dad worked
for the city, and our drinking water came
from the sewers. He knew.

I read we're 50% water,
no, 70%,
NO! A full 90%.
We're basically puddles with legs.

Jesus turned water to wine,
gave us a sip, and said *Enjoy!*
But not too much.
It was so much better than water, but
everyone's saying we need
to drink more water, so
we fumble for our nightstands and
down as much as we can at 4 a.m.

One girl drank so much water
she tipped the ratio and died.
It's all anyone can talk about at school.

Water is bad for you, they say.
You can drown in it.

In eighth grade, we learn that
pool is *piscine* in French.
"Don't piscine the pool," says the guy
with the greasiest hair and the
saggiest sweatpants.

I read Virginia Woolf, and
how she drowned herself in the River Ouse.
I read *The Waves* and splash around in
the idea that every life is
just a drop in an ocean of dinosaur piss.

I wake up every morning in
sweaty sheets. A little bit more of me
dripped out, staining the pillowcase.
117 billion people have lived and died
in this whole tear-streaked world.
Billions of dirty little drops
clinging to Yeti bottles and
foggy windows at Makeout Point.
Over two-thirds of the planet is water, but
just try and make me take a sip
that hasn't kissed a coffee bean
or taken a long bath in some barley.

ATTRITION

Can you just listen to this, I ask the husband
as he puts on his boots
to go cut something on a sawhorse.
He says yes
with a sigh
that perhaps only I can hear.
I hurry through it, because
when the poem's done and
he's nodded, said yeah it's good,
then I can sit and think
oh well,
poetry's not for everyone.

With him outside,
I can go on writing,
believing I am unread
only because poetry's dead,
and he can make a crooked birdhouse
that will only ever house
black widows and dry rot.

We live in a trailer
in a small town, and
really who gives a fuck that
we never made it?
One day, my unread poems,
the birdhouse,
and the Parthenon
will all be rubble
sailing off into space.
The sun will grow cold
and everything will stop.
And the tiny sigh

the husband refused to let out, yet
couldn't quite keep in,
won't hurt even a little.

MAGGOTS

There are only five or so things
to fill out an evening, and
none of them are that great
sober. Sitting alone
after another day
trying so damn hard not to snack or
eat too much, trying
to get off my ass and
walk the same old trails, only to
watch the hours tick from 6:45
to 7:01 to suddenly 8:39 with no good plans...
It was inevitable as an affair between
two people stranded on an island.

Me and my stupid aching want
got in the car and went to buy beer.
Me and my loneliness drank
four or five in not very long and
started grating cheese and
frying things and playing music too loud,
watching the beginnings of
five or six shows before settling on
something I've seen enough times
I didn't have to pay attention.

Sometimes, like tonight,
I'll bring myself to do things I can't do
when I'm of sound mind.
Tonight, I cleaned out the fridge.

As I moved a Tupperware of
weeks-old pasta to the trash,
a single maggot fell out and lay
curling, screaming silently

on the floor.
I ripped a piece of paper towel,
stooped over it, picked up its rotten,
useless life, and squeezed.

TRAILER PARKS

Walking into the trailer park, it's easy
      to become unstuck
      from the rest of the world.
The people are slower here,
      moving like street performers
      dipped in brass.
There's the man with the pot belly
      watering the driveway. The oil stains
      aren't moving and the cracks need filling.
      It's 2 p.m. and he's not at work, but
      the water's slopping
      from the end of his faded hose.

There's the Saint Bernard or the Bernise or the
      hundred-pound thing you couldn't name
      jumping behind the chain-link fence, roaring, bellowing,
      intent on ripping out your throat.

Somebody hollers from another trailer,
      a woman's voice, a shrill falsetto layered with
      the grinding, mechanical groan of her voice box
      spinning its wheels in tar.

There's the trailer with the sagging addition,
      siding buckling like a button-up over a beer gut,
      eavestroughs full of last year's leaves,
      the hint of a tarp like too little wrapping paper
      trying to hold it all together.

There's the Live Laugh Love over a tattered screen door and
      another and another,
      hung like dollar-store wreaths.

The people are pale and doughy,
        squished into people shapes by
        thrift-store clothes that walk around
        like the ghosts of their previous owners.
Their eyes are empty and their yards full.

You walk past them to your own trailer,
        forgetting their faces
        as you close the door.
Once inside, you are just a person cooking dinner,
        doing the laundry,
        reading a poem,
        drinking wine on a Tuesday –
        a person just like any of them.

BOB AND JAN

Their trailer has been moved three times.
Not because the property lines have shifted,
but because they were never right to begin with,
and the new neighbours have grown weary
of their rambling ways.

"I've been recovering all year," she says
around a cigarette whose long ash
refuses to obey anyone's laws.

"From what?" you ask before you can stop yourself.
"Well, the mastectomy," she croaks.
You say you didn't notice anything off
about her body, which is shaped
like a bag of leaves,
leaving out that it's because
her body draws the eye about as much
as a bag of leaves.

You sit on your country porch to read, and
Bon Jovi competes
over the endless hollering
of her latest beau
who stands on the front lawn in hoodie and shorts,
cheap beer in a chalky fist that
might have worked up north or
never at all.

They offer to mow your lawn, give you a beer,
walk the dog if you're gone all day.
They only leave to fill jerry cans
or restock the fridge in the back.

"I'm so glad you moved in," Jan says
as you empty the trunk.
"The people before were so rude."

You recall your mom's warning to
never feed a stray as
Bob revs an unseen quad and hollers,
"Who wants to go for a ride?"

Unincorporated

The town is a sprawl of shabby brick bungalows and
empty baseball diamonds huddled around a
concrete company and a handful of filthy garages.

Strewn along the highway like garbage,
the town was only incorporated due to a population boom
when a mine briefly opened a generation or two earlier.

It was once the site of a great battle
between warring Indigenous tribes. Now
you can buy keychains and ashtrays with
red faces and the names of long-dead heroes
at the last gas station out of town.

The windows of the last mom-and-pops
are littered with yellowing pleas for help
finding daughters, sisters, mothers.
Under ads for local limb removal, garbage pickup,
and safe walk groups, the flyers flap in the breeze.
They fade in the summer sun, get soaked
in autumn rain, freeze, thaw, and fade some more,
but they're never taken down.
The townspeople lumber by, oblivious, on their way
to the credit union, the Elks Hall, the liquor store.

Meanwhile, with more hitchhikers than cars,
the garages close on weekends, then finally
for good. The houses go unpainted with
no grandkids to impress, and the ball fields,
long bereft of cheers and the crack of bat on ball,
grow over. Only the concrete factory limps along,
pumping out headstones and
patching potholes.

DIARRHEA HONEYMOON

If you ever want to really be known,
to share your innermost parts with another human –
what makes you sweat, the things you'll say
when the pressure's on – try contracting
explosive diarrhea
in a honeymoon suite in Cuba.
Bonus points if it's a small suite with
no fan in the bathroom to muffle the screams.

In a country like Cuba where soap
is a basement religion with a secret handshake,
and toilet seats and TP are little more than
papered-over propaganda from an old regime,
it's not hard to let things slide a little.
Sadly, the only Os here are the ones
that sometimes pop up in the spelling of diarrhoea.
Round and resolute, they sit on the Imodium and the
Pepto boxes like the pursed lips at the end of *I do*.

Finally, as a married person, you get to learn
the dark secrets of what goes on behind the
closed doors of married people. You'll make out first-hand
the muffled sounds and shuffles, the slap of flesh
on flesh, or flesh on floor, as the feet tap out
an SOS on the cold tiles in front of the toilet.
Like the debt of climate change and
so many other kinds of debt, this world is now yours.

To open up your dark and dirty little insides and
splash around together in the stank of two people
breathing the same air, warm with love – such is the gift
of sharing your life. To burnish the porcelain sheen of youth
with real-world experience, such is it to be loved.

Wade through the river of a sexless honeymoon,
and you will find yourself on the shore
of someplace truly new.

GRANDMA IN THE NURSING HOME

The old bodies – stale,
piss-smelling, ingrown hairs,
yellow nails – are propped in chairs,
silver eyes open to the floor.
The machine that checks blood pressure,
the yellow pill bottles,
the white hair curled as if for a dance,
the button-up shirts and overalls
fighting gravity, pulling the pants up and away
from the bony fingers in the dirt –
I weave through it all to Grandma.
She's slouched at her table, but
so much more a person than these grey
forgotten ornaments waiting to shatter
if someone steps on them.
She doesn't belong here, but
ninety-nine years is a long time to breathe in
and out, and she's grown tired of in.
"This is my granddaughter," she says
to the dead-eyed ladies. I button her bib
and kiss the warm tissue paper
of her wrinkled cheek.

A nurse tells me visitors need to leave, and
I feel like shouting,
"That's my grandmother in there –
the only one I have left! She used to bake
a hundred loaves of bread and
muck the stalls before the sun came up.
She always hugged me and palmed me fifty, but
it wasn't about buying my visits –
we both knew from day one that
the world was hard, and we needed to help
those we loved when we could."

Instead, I give Grandma a kiss,
promise to see her next week.
"That's my granddaughter,"
she says again as I leave, and
even from a few tables away,
keys jingling in my hand,
I hear the smile in her voice.

THE FIREPLACE

The fireplace is a pine box that sits in our living room.
It used to sit in my grandma's.
It doesn't burn wood like real fireplaces,
or gas or coal or anything at all.
What happens is, you flick a button
and a rod with metal flaps rotates,
reflecting the light from a light bulb.
Two fake logs smoulder,
but they never go out.
It's like a fireplace, but it is not
a fireplace. It's dandruff on a fireplace's shoulder,
the empty woodshed that still smells like split pine.

I read somewhere that when you're cremated
your teeth can burst from the heat.
But my grandma had no teeth of her own
so at least she avoided that.

My fireplace doesn't always give heat.
You can choose different settings.
Tonight, almost mid-September,
it's too warm for even a blanket,
but with the fan on my face and the window open,
I turn the heat on low and smell the dust
burning on the grill.

LOOK TO THE SPOUSE

The pandemic is still in full swing, but
with the heat and boredom and summer vacation
spilling its sandy bounty all over our toes,
most of us are a little lax with the rules.
Take yesterday, for example.
It was Father's Day *and* the day after my birthday.
My whole life, my family and I have celebrated
both occasions together. To avoid such a party just because
half a million people have died seemed...
Well, honestly, it wasn't even discussed.

My sixty-two-year-old mom was there,
and my sixty-year-old dad. My sisters were there
and their sweet little girls, aged two and one.
The two most vulnerable categories of human –
excusing those with chronic illness – and
no one wore masks. We sat inside,
facing each other around a table.
Only soap, water, and luck stood between us
and death, according to the news.

How ironic that those we love most
are the ones we place most squarely in danger.

Like the murder porn proves again and again, though –
when in doubt as to who could commit the worst,
most brutal crimes,
it's always best to
look to the spouse.

Piss Poems

I read a poem about the time
Bukowski's drunk woman
pissed in the elevator.
And I thought of the time
I read a poem to a room full of people
that began: *the best piss I ever took*
was beneath the Eiffel Tower.
I was in love with that line, and
after I said it, I lingered for
the *ooohs* and *ahhs* that
would surely come.

No one said much of anything,
so I just kept reading.

And in that moment, I suddenly knew
that talking about a piss you took
is neither shocking
nor poetry.

Everyone has pissed.
Everyone has thought
I am pissing as they pissed.
Everyone has heard other people pissing
from the next stall over and thought
that person is pissing.
No one is shocked by
the thought of piss.

You could always say
I convalesced beneath the Eiffel Tower.
At least people might look up the meaning
of *convalescence*
and maybe learn something new.

And then you'd have an argument on your hands.
Some folks would say
you used it properly,
while others would say the opposite.
And then you'd have literature.

To Freeze

It's minus 15 out,
mid-pandemic.
Outside isn't safe.
Inside isn't safe, so
I am in the car,
which is nowhere,
driving around town,
looking at buildings
like a giant
too big to fit inside.

The one tiny patch of lake not frozen
is thrashing in the cutting wind –
annoyed to be so cold
and unable to freeze.

I wish I had more time
and less time
and a word for that feeling.

I wish words could do more
than point to all the problems
and give them names.

RINGS

Before my grandma died
we took all her furniture
and placed her in a home.
She was hallucinating and terrifying
everyone close to her.
Her furniture – the kitchen set and the coffee table
and the nightstand where her Bible sat –
were stowed on people's porches
and in sheds. Good, quality stuff
she used for most of her life
to host dinners, hold her clothes,
sit beneath bowls of chips on holidays or
when we bothered to visit.

The coffee table that I took from her things
and use to hold my beer and coffee
is ringed and dusty. Grandma never drank
or allowed dust to settle on anything she cared for.
I'm always careful to wipe it down
when I think of it, but
the rings have melded into the wood grains
and can't be wiped away.

Grandma worked fifteen years in a warehouse,
on her feet all day, saving good fruit
for the families of the valley and
tossing out the rotten.

I sit here every day,
getting paid to study poetry,
each day adding
a few more rings to her furniture.

I spoke at her funeral, and
though I'd have traded
all the furniture and beer and poems
just to have her back,
it still felt good to be told, afterwards,
how great my speech was,
and to be asked if I couldn't use a beer
after all that hard work.

NATURE LOVERS

You've gone and bought six lobelia seedlings,
which means you're about to tell me
I don't love Nature like you do.

I do love Nature, I say. I love being
in it, love walking in the trees.
Just because I don't need to make it myself –

You cut me off with a romantic line about
hands in sand and how I'm happy just looking
out a window. I'm not, of course, but
my words mean nothing to you with
no soil under my nails. Loving Nature and
being project-oriented are different, I say,
my face red like an indoor tan on dry skin.

More of the same, then we're silent and
you're outside in Nature's unknowable embrace,
lining up your plants like
budding trophies.

I hate when it's over, you holler
over your seedlings' heads and through the open window.
It's just like,
oh my god, GROW.

The Pillars

In teacher training, they told us all about the girl who was fired for posting a selfie holding a beer on her Facebook page. They told us about the man who lost his job after arguing with the neighbour about a tree overlapping their property lines. You are always on, they said. Even when you're not in the classroom, you must set an example. You're a pillar of the community now, and if there's a crack in a single pillar, the whole structure will collapse. I thought about all the cracked places in my life – the years of beers well-documented, the low-cut dresses, my ass – what place did any of those have in the load-bearing of public minds? The stories of those who'd actually touched kids came out and we hundreds in the auditorium all shook our heads. Not us, we all knew. Not the pillars. Pillars do nothing but stand still and support those who need to lean against something, or be protected. Maybe we just won't drink anymore, some of us said. That's fine, they said. Just don't let anyone fall behind or feel left out. The world is cruel, but school shouldn't be. That's just fine, we all said. We agree with that. But tell us – how do we actually teach? How do you what now? they said.

SELF PORTRAIT

I'm not a conservative
    but, like,
    I spank my dog
    when she barks
    at the cars on the highway.
I'm not a liberal either
    but I carry my poetry to the beach
    in a *New Yorker* tote I got before
    I cancelled my subscription.

I don't have a subscription anywhere.
    I read the same four books and
    watch the same four movies over and over.

I write in the style of whatever poet
    I'm reading
    on whatever day.

The only things I really have are
    beer and telling everyone I think
    I should stop drinking
    so much beer, before they can tell me
    to stop drinking
so much beer.

PLUSH EMOJIS

Red light at a desolate intersection
forces my handmade purse to the floor.
I look to see who I hate this time.
It's a man in a "that guy" truck and trailer
smoking with his windows up.
He glances at me – not to gloat, but because
my shoulders are bare.

Morning coffee in the mall before the stores open;
people-watching as the grey-hairs discuss
gluten, the kids, the times.
– *It's so much worse out there these days.*
– *These godless millennials.*
– *I blame cell phones.*

The FedEx man waits for the girl in Old Navy to
open the gate. The man from UPS does the same
with the girl at the import store. I am in a dress, but I feel radical
accepting no man's delivery while
awash in discount tees.

Plastic bubbles sit in a vending machine
crammed full of plush emojis,
adding chance to parody.
How do I feel today? Here's a toonie and a faux metal crank.

I step outside to feed the meter.
Fuck the Police is plastered over the coin slot.
I feel no comradeship with this bid for anarchy.
Mine is a clean day of well-trod dreams
and little more. A sign on the highway tells me
the lines on the road are being painted;

I need to turn left,
but I wait until the signs are gone
and the still unpainted lines go with them,
        and the sidewalks with those.

ACKNOWLEDGMENTS

Thank you so much to Denis De Klerck for saying yes; to Stuart Ross for the incredible support editing and helping me realize what this book could be; to Michael V. Smith for reading this collection first, for teaching me so many invaluable things about poetry, and for encouraging me to publish; to Marshall Reeves for always challenging and loving me; to Kirstina Klausmayer for her unwavering support, enthusiasm, and friendship; to my family, without whom I would be nothing at all, much less a poet; to Brittany Ferguson for always reading my work and texting back "Ooo I love that!"; to Catherine Cohen, who writes whatever the hell she wants, and who reminded me I could, too; to my wonderful friend and travel buddy, Laura Sciarpelletti, who's always waiting at the terminal when I need her most; to Andisha Sabri Carey, who jumped at the chance to collaborate, and without whom several of these poems would not exist; to my many friends and profs who've opened my eyes in so many ways; and lastly, thank you to the many desk jobs that gave me so much material and time to write.

Many of these poems first appeared in various forms within *Jokes Review, Minola Review, Wage Slaves: An Anthology of the Underemployed, Dusie, Leaping Clear, The HitchLit Review, Tenth Street Miscellany*, and *Outlook Springs*, and I would like to thank the editors for giving my poetry its first breath in this world.

Brianna Ferguson is a writer from the Okanagan Valley in British Columbia. A current MFA candidate at the University of British Columbia, she also holds a BA in Creative Writing and a BEd in Secondary Education from UBC. Her poems and stories have appeared in various publications across North America and the U.K. *A Nihilist Walks into a Bar* is her first book.